My Life as an OAK TREE

by John Sazaklis

illustrated by Bonnie Pang

Hi, there! As you can see, I am an oak tree! You look very familiar. We might have met on a walk through the park. Or maybe you've seen me in your own backyard!

My Life Cycle

My Life as an OAK TREE

PICTURE WINDOW BOOKS
a capstone imprint

Published by Picture Window Books, an imprint of Capstone
1710 Roe Crest Drive, North Mankato, Minnesota 56003
capstonepub.com

Library of Congress Cataloging-in-Publication Data
Names: Sazaklis, John, author. | Pang, Bonnie, illustrator.
Title: My life as an oak tree / by John Sazaklis ; illustrated by Bonnie Pang.
Description: North Mankato, Minnesota : Picture Window Books, [2022] | Series: My life cycle | Includes index. | Audience: Ages 5–7 | Audience: Grades K–1 | Summary: "Hi, there! I'm an oak tree. You might see me everywhere, but have you ever stopped to think about how I got there? Learn more about my life cycle and how I went from a tiny little acorn to a big, beautiful tree."—Provided by publisher.
Identifiers: LCCN 2021022058 (print) | LCCN 2021022059 (ebook) |
  ISBN 9781663984838 (hardcover) | ISBN 9781666332421 (pdf) |
  ISBN 9781666332445 (kindle edition)
Subjects: LCSH: Oak—Life cycles—Juvenile literature.
Classification: LCC QK495.F14 S29 2022 (print) | LCC QK495.F14 (ebook) | DDC 583/.65—dc23
LC record available at https://lccn.loc.gov/2021022058
LC ebook record available at https://lccn.loc.gov/2021022059

Editorial Credits
Editor: Alison Deering; Designer: Kay Fraser; Media Researcher: Svetlana Zhurkin;
Production Specialist: Katy LaVigne

Printed and bound in the USA. 4608

I might look big and strong to you now, but I didn't start out that way. Do you know how I got here? The story is quite nuts—*literally*!

It all started with a little nut called an acorn. I grow them right here on my body! That's called **fruiting**.

STALK

CUP OF
SCALES

NUT

SEED

Want to hear something *really* impressive? I can make as many as 10 million acorns in my lifetime!

Inside the acorn is a seed full of **nutrients**, which is lots of good food needed to grow. My acorns are so tasty that these furry little thieves called squirrels try to steal them! But I have a secret scheme to stop their sneaky snack attacks.

Acorns need to be underground to grow. So, do you know what I do? I drop them on the ground—*oops!*—and those silly squirrels scoop them right up.

They like to bury their stolen goods in the dirt, to store them away for the winter months. But that just makes the acorns grow faster. Mission accomplished!

Once it's underground, the seed inside the acorn starts to **germinate**. Then my **taproot** breaks free! It pokes through the nut's shell and digs straight down, deep into the dirt.

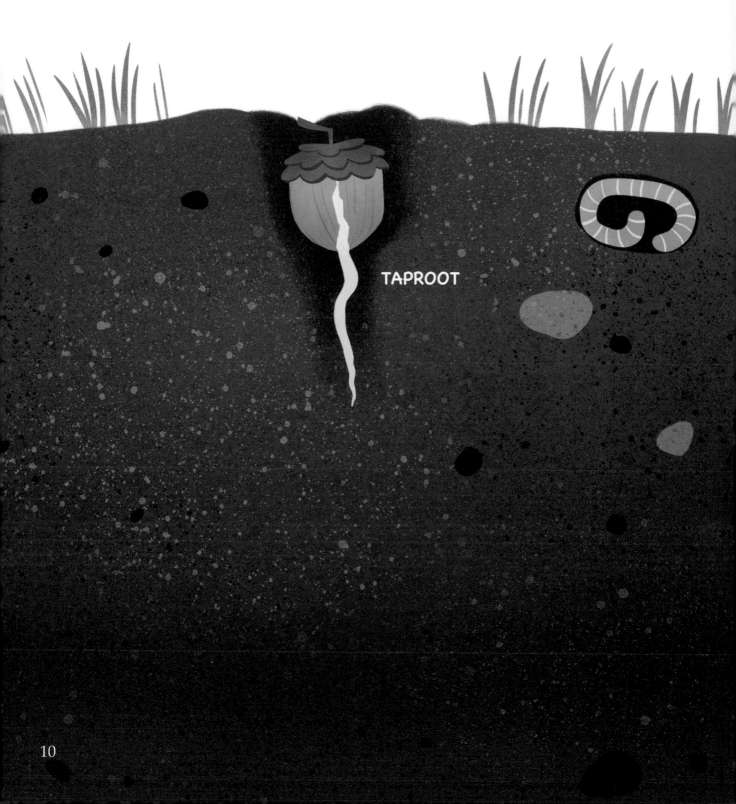

TAPROOT

Other **roots** start to grow out sideways. I call those my root troop! Roots suck up water and nutrients from the soil. SLURP!

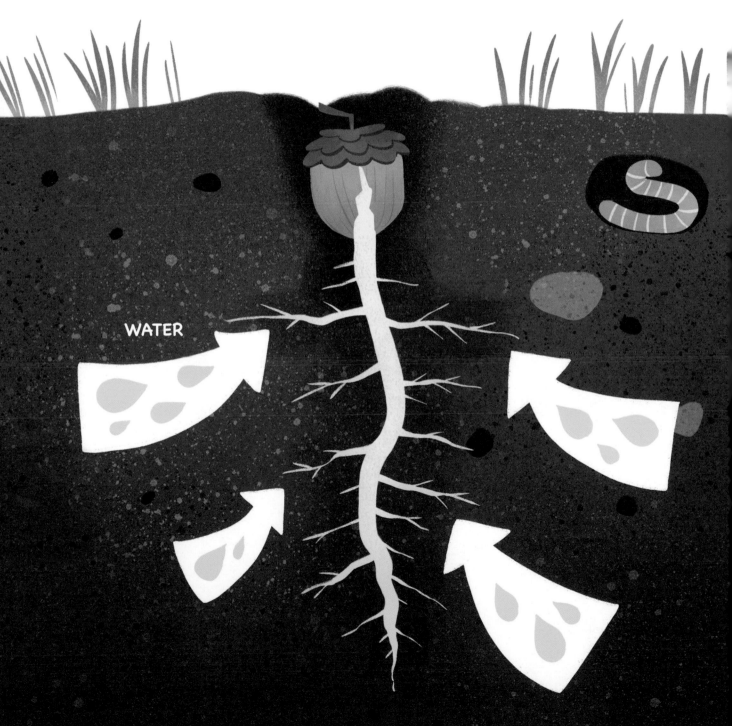

WATER

After about three weeks, a **sprout** appears above ground. This is my announcement to the world: LOOK AT ME—I'M A FUTURE TREE!

I still have more growing to do, though. It takes about three and a half months for my sprout to become a **seedling**.

A seedling is made of three parts: a root, a **shoot**, and a **leaf**. Now, the root you've already met, but let me introduce you to its *extended* family. I'm serious—they extend out from the root!

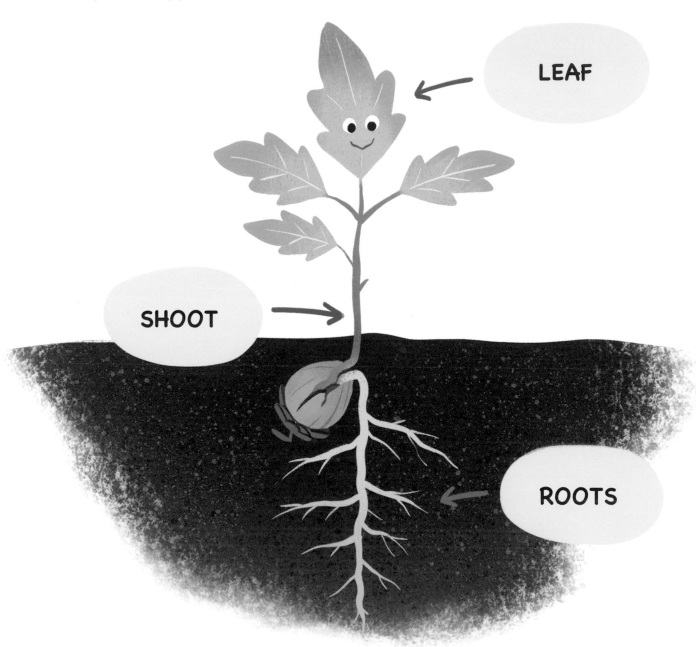

First up is the shoot. It sucks water up from my root and spreads it to my leaf.

Last but not least,
we have the leaf.
It **absorbs** the warm
rays from the sun.
That helps give me
the energy I need
to keep growing.

After about five years, I have a super growth spurt! WOO-HOO!
Time for me to make the leap from a seedling to a **sapling**.

But the bad news is, I'm now at that awkward in-between stage . . . also known as the teenage years. I'm going to be stuck here for five to six years. Ugh! *So* embarrassing!

As a sapling, I have a thicker shoot, which is really a thin trunk. My branches are gangly, and my leaves are patchy.

I haven't reached my full potential—or height—yet. I am only about 3 feet (1 meter) tall. That makes me the perfect height for woodland creatures to nibble on my leaves. Excuse me, deer. Please *leaf* me alone! OUCH!

As I grow older, my trunk becomes thicker and rougher.
These layers and layers of dead tree cells are called **bark**.
Hmm . . . maybe that's why dogs like trees so much!

By the time I'm 15 years old, I'm about 10 feet (3 m) tall. I can't make acorns—yet—but I can provide homes for birds and squirrels.

I enjoy the company, but I do *not* enjoy when uninvited mushrooms appear. There is nothing *fun* about fungus!

People like me too—and they always have! Did you know that in ancient Greece, the oak tree was the symbol of Zeus, king of the gods?

Hundreds of years later, the Vikings used my wood to build their ships. After that, my wood was used to build shelter and furniture. Not to brag, but I'm kind of a big deal.

Speaking of big, I'm finally an adult tree! It only took 20 to 30 years—sometimes more. I can grow to be 60 to 100 feet (18 to 30 m) tall.

I'm still young compared to some of my relatives, though. The Great Oak, known as Wi'áaşal by the Pechanga people, put down roots in California and is more than 1,000 years old.

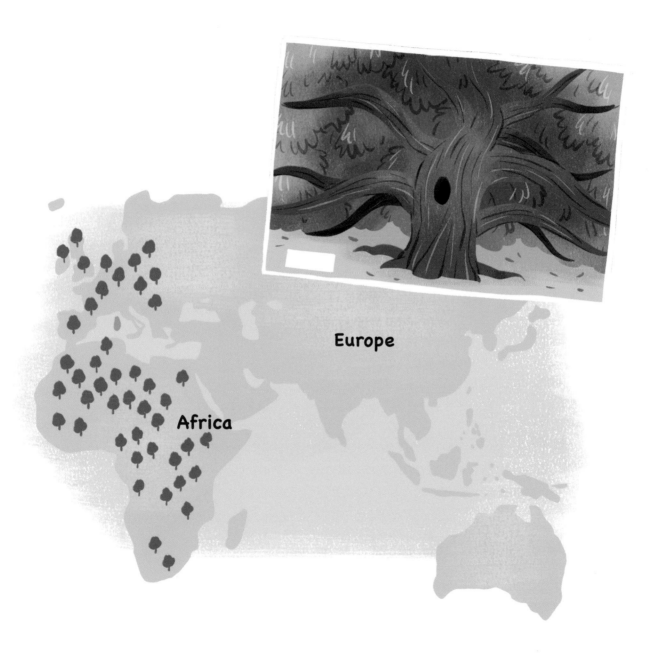

I have cousins in Europe and Africa too. We have been on Earth for millions of years. Do you remember where we came from?

The acorn! That's right. I'm sure you've heard the saying:
If an acorn falls in the forest, does it make a sound?

It doesn't matter . . . it's going to make an oak tree. HA!

My Life as an Oak Tree

About the Author

John Sazaklis is a *New York Times* bestselling author with more than 100 children's books under his utility belt! He has also illustrated Spider-Man books, created toys for *MAD* magazine, and written for the *BEN 10* animated series. John lives in New York City with his superpowered wife and daughter.

About the Illustrator

Bonnie Pang is an illustrator and comic artist from Hong Kong. She currently illustrates children's books and creates the webcomic *IT Guy & ART Girl*. When not drawing, she enjoys watching movies, gardening, and exploring new places.

Glossary

absorb (ab-ZORB)—to soak up

bark (BARK)—the hard covering on the outside of a tree

fruit (FROOT)—to bear fruit

germinate (JUR-muh-neyt)—when a seed sends out a root and a stem and begins to grow into a new plant

leaf (LEEF)—the flat and usually green part of a plant that grows out from a stem

nutrients (NOO-tree-uhnts)—parts of food, like vitamins, that are used for growth

root (ROOT)—the part of the plant that is underground

sapling (SAP-ling)—a young tree

seedling (SEED-ling)—a young plant

shoot (SHOOT)—the white stem growing out of a seed that becomes a plant

sprout (SPROWT)—a young plant that has just appeared above the soil

taproot (TAP-root)—the large main root of a plant from which smaller roots grow

Index